SIX STEPS TO NOT WORK

SOMEONE ELSE'S DREAM

The Guide to Unlocking Your

Path to Riches

Mon De Leseo Williams

1

INTRODUCTION

We all can become rich. No matter where you were born, no matter the color of your skin, no matter your gender, no matter what religion or beliefs you hold dear, everyone has that chance. Some have a few obstacles in their way, others have thousands, some were given a helping hand, and others must work it out all alone. However, the chance is there for all. Once you realize this, it becomes a question of how you recognize your wealth, what your first steps will be, and how you maintain the needed drive.

Let me show you.

CONTENTS

ACKNOWLEDGMENTS

First and foremost, I would love to thank God. I would also love to say thank you to Pastor Jeremy Leech; you told me to never be afraid to fail. And thanks to my team because this work would not have been possible without you.

CHAPTER ONE

Realizing Wealth Is Possible

Are you thriving financially? Do you have enough money to take care of your needs? Do you have enough money to go on vacations with your family as you wish? Are your savings and investments increasing? Do you have cash put away for a rainy day? If you answered "NO" to any of these questions, it is time you admit to yourself that you suck with money. However, no matter how much you are struggling today, unimaginable wealth is always possible if you take the right steps. Let's be honest, if you were not born rich, then you were likely never brought up with the mind-set that becoming wealthy was possible. You grew up with the wrong information about earning money and about managing cash. Therefore, it is time to unlearn everything you think you know about money, business, investments, and savings. Start from scratch with new lessons and a new mentality. Anything is achievable if you put your mind to it and apply it to your daily life. Without committing your entire being to a project, it has no hope of getting off the ground. Essentially, unless you are thriving with several digits in your bank account(s), you obviously need help with money management.

Not everyone is born with the same opportunities. Some were born into wealth, whereas others were born into poverty. Some were handed money at an early age, whereas others had to work for it. However, although opportunities from birth are different, everyone has the same chance to become rich. Wealth is achievable for every person on the planet. Some must work far harder for it, but that makes it all the sweeter when you get there. The critical thing to get your head around is that having $100,000 in your account is not a dream and becoming a millionaire is not a fairy tale.

I'm quite sure you hear the stories about self-made millionaires in the news all the time—people who come up with that one killer idea or who have mastered the art of one kind of trade and made millions. These people pick something they are good at and invest time, effort, and emotion until it becomes profitable. Others simply come up with excuses, claiming that they were not born into wealth, so it is an unachievable goal. That way of thinking is lazy. Humanity would never evolve and thrive if everyone on the planet had this mind-set. Be prepared to push the boundaries and become exceptional. Be driven toward becoming the person others look up to. Motivate other people to follow your journey to the top. Success and money are waiting for you at the top of the ladder. You must be prepared to haul yourself to the top, no matter what!

CHAPTER TWO

Driving Yourself to Success

If you are aiming to become a success story, it is about living every single day with the mind-set of getting to the top. There are no off days on your journey. You should push yourself, grow, and look for new opportunities to earn big money with every passing hour. Those who sit back and wait for the money to come to them will never make it big in this world. You must be proactive and brave and think big to see that money rolling into your bank account. Be motivated every single day. You can rest when you're sleeping on a bed of cash. For now, you need to put in the extra effort to ensure you have a cash-loaded future.

How do you keep yourself motivated? The answer is simple: goals. Merely saying to yourself, "I want to be a millionaire in five years," doesn't make it a reality. You need to think about the short term before you dream of the long term. Motivate yourself by setting small goals across a short period of time. Buy yourself a notebook, and jot down your goals for the week. What do you want to achieve in the next seven days? How will you reach these goals? How will these goals help you in the long run? Then, write down your goals for the month, the quarter, the year, and beyond. Make sure your goals are specific, measurable, achievable, realistic, and time bound (SMART). Map out your journey to the top, and strictly follow your goals. By doing this, you will most certainly carve a path to your riches. Nothing comes by luck; it comes from cash management and thorough planning.

Save yourself a dollar a day for five years. This may sound like a ridiculous amount, but by the time a half-decade passes, you will be sitting on thousands. Better yet, put away $100 per month for five years, and watch the total rise. Even this will not pave a path to riches for you, but it will provide you with a starting point: $6,000. This will not change your life on its own. You will not consider yourself rich if you have $6,000 in the bank. However, if you have $6,000, you can invest in a money-making opportunity instantly. You can purchase something that will appreciate, and watch the $6,000 climb to ten, then twenty, fifty, one hundred, and beyond. The $6,000 is simply your starting point, the beginning of your journey.

Finally, although it may sound like a strange tip, eat healthy foods. Eating and drinking healthy keeps the mind clear. It keeps you fit, it helps you maintain a positive attitude, and it has you firing on all cylinders. A healthy mind is one step closer to a

healthy bank account.

CHAPTER THREE

The First Step to Wealth

So, how do you take your first step toward wealth? Once you believe in yourself and are confident that you can become rich with the right mind-set and decisions, it is all about implementing those beliefs in the real world. Almost every single person on the planet lives above their means, but what does that mean exactly? Most of us run and jump over the line between necessity and luxury. Think back over your past week. Did you go out for a drink? Did you pay for an expensive meal? Did you treat yourself to some online shopping? Maybe you purchased a new video game or went to the movies? How many things can you count that you spent money on but did not need? Now, calculate how much cost you incurred buying those items; you will be surprised at how much cash you spend on frivolous items. Habits drain pockets, and expensive habits cripple you financially. This is like locking your tires while expecting your car to run smoothly and hit its top speed. You are shooting yourself in the foot before you have even started.

Think of it like this: those pleasures and habits are luxuries you cannot afford at the moment. However, you can afford all these things when you are rich. Once you earn your wealth, you will have more than enough money to spend on whatever you enjoy while maintaining your bank balance. However, when starting from the bottom, every little bit counts. You can't make investments without any cash. You need to be strict with yourself and dedicate every spare penny toward your financial future if you are to have any hope of achieving the wealth of your dreams. Instead of spending the cash on an expensive meal, save by shopping at a discount store and looking for the best deals, so you can cook at home. Instead of buying a new wardrobe, repurpose your old clothes or check out bargain shops. Instead of going to the movies, watch a DVD at home. You can save every day, and even the smallest amount of savings piles up.

You also need to invest; look for things that appreciate. Instead of treating yourself to a new car that instantly loses value once it leaves the showroom, spend your money on something more worthy of your time: stocks, watches, artwork, property, and anything else that goes up in value over the years for a smooth turnaround. You only have to buy it, wait for it to become more valuable, and then sell it for a sweet profit. What could be easier? Once you have made a few successful investments, you can spend your money on something bigger and better, bringing in a healthier return. Before you know it, you'll be a real estate tycoon with houses all over the country and multiple digits stacking up in your bank account!

CHAPTER FOUR

Invest in Self-Improvement

Succeeding is as much about what's on the inside as it is about what you accomplish on the outside. If you are not healthy within, then you can never increase the health of your business and bank account. Think of it like this: an investment in yourself and your well-being is also an investment in your business. You are the business; you are the brains. Without you, the operation does not run like a well-oiled machine. Therefore, ensure that you are a well-oiled machine. But how do you do this?

Education

Business is a knowledge game. Therefore, investing in your education is a fantastic way to invest in your success. It always pays to increase your knowledge base and update your skills, learning new things from people who had been there and done that. You can achieve this several ways, whether via a business university course, an online course, seminars, books written by experts, or anything else along those lines. Any time you are taking tried and tested knowledge and committing it to memory, you are investing well in your business.

Eating Habits

This one may sound a bit confusing. However, eating habits can have significant effects on your business. As explained above, you are the brain behind the operation. You are also likely the person who attends important meetings with all potential clients and partners, works long hours, and keeps the ship moving, which requires a lot of energy. It is a known fact that eating a well-balanced and healthy diet improves your mood, energy, and ability to work. Therefore, why would you not give yourself these little boosts?

Exercise

Everything pointed out above can also be said about exercise. A fit body is a fit mind. Keep yourself active and healthy to maintain a positive attitude and plenty of get-up-and-go!

Find a Mentor

You cannot expect to walk into a new business, industry, or market and instantly become an expert. It takes years of training, learning, and hands-on experience to give yourself that title. However, the next best thing beyond becoming an instant expert is hiring one. Find yourself a mentor to guide you through the process, especially in the early stages. This will give you a steady hand to steer the ship while you learn the ropes yourself. Who knows, one day someone might ask you to do the same for them; that is the goal.

Meditate

Clear your brain with calming and relaxing meditations. This can relieve stress, prevent overthinking, and open your mind to new possibilities. It promotes positive attitudes, which is everything in business.

Get More Sleep

Many people will tell you that business is all about sleepless nights and putting in extra effort. Yes, put your all into your work, but there must be boundaries. Working while tired equals crappy work and an increased chance of mistakes. Set yourself consistent working hours, and put all your endeavor into that time. However, once it is time to sleep, go to bed. You should aim for 7–8 hours daily of sleep to ensure you maintain maximum output potential.

Stop Procrastinating

Work on one task at a time. Once you take on too much work and too many jobs, your mind begins to burn out, and you start to procrastinate. However, by making a plan and working within it, you give yourself a sense of progress that keeps you driving on.

Manage Your Time

Develop a routine and stick to it. Take a day to plan the perfect daily schedule for you and your work. This schedule should be efficient, making the best use of your time consistently. Once you have a detailed schedule, it becomes a matter of training yourself to follow it every day until it becomes a pattern you are comfortable with.

CHAPTER FIVE

Find Your Talent and Make the Most of It

One of the most asked questions about business is, how do you find that jackpot money-making opportunity? Well, there is one key and simple answer to this question: you don't. You should not be actively seeking money-making shortcuts; instead, you should look for a topic or industry that gets you excited.

Ask yourself:

- What excites you?

- What hobbies do you have?

- What are you good at?

- What are your main talents?

- What did you excel at in school?

- Would you consider yourself an expert on anything?

- What subject do you know more about than the average person?

These questions should lead you to one subject or topic or activity. Whether that may be your favorite sport, the art of writing, selling goods, or designing websites, it simply doesn't matter. When you feel excited, your heart is racing, and it doesn't feel like work, then it is your ideal opportunity. This is your golden ticket to success!

A huge part of the business is the passion you put into every decision you make and every conversation you take part in. If you do not believe in your product or service, then how could you possibly expect anyone else to? Not only should you be an expert in your field, but you should be happy to talk about it until the cows come home.

Now that you have chosen your subject, use your natural excitement and take advantage of it. Research everything there is to know about that subject. Let's take the art of writing as an example. If you are a keen writer, you could take the time to research the world of publishing, what literary agents do, how to write a book, and how to market a book. Everything that is remotely related to your area of choice is a potential knowledge bank to be slurped up. If you were not an expert before, then you should be now!

Now comes the moneymaker. You can take your subject of expertise, the subject that excites you, and you can discover how to make money out of it. How many ways can you think of to turn your avocation into cash? Let's continue with that writing example. If you were passionate about writing, you could do the following:

- Become a freelance writer.
- Publish a book and sell it.

- Teach the art of writing.

- Start a publishing company.

- Start a literary house and become an agent.

- Start a book printing company.

- Start a book marketing company.

- Start a book cover design company.

- Design an online course on the art of writing and publishing.

This is a list I came up with in no more than a minute. The truth is that if you are excited and passionate enough about a subject, there is always money to be made from it!

CHAPTER SIX

Spend Money Like Rich People

When you start earning a lot of money, you must know how to spend wisely. No one has ever become rich off the back of silly and frivolous spending. Anyone who has earned their wealth, rather than being born to it, knows this simple fact. So, how should you manage your spending habits?

Save/Invest More Than You Spend

You should always save or invest more money each month than you spend on yourself. Let's say you earn $1,000 a month. You should be looking to save or invest at least 50–60% of this, if not more. The general rule, especially early in your business or your journey to success, should be to spend only when you need to. Anything that does not fall into that necessity bracket should go straight into savings or investments.

Self-Control

A lot of saving and investing comes down to self-control. Can you walk past a shop with the new gadget or item of clothing you want without having to go in and buy it? Can you sensibly weigh a decision in your head and determine whether you need something? If you are frivolous with your spending, you will find your savings drop further and further away from where you need them to be. Once you get caught in a spiral of spending, it's hard to stop. Thankfully, once you train yourself to cut back on spending, it becomes a habit.

Invest in a Product

Do you have money to spare at the end of the month? Invest in extra product or inventory for your business. Putting money back into your business is a surefire way to grow and get more money out in the long run.

If It Isn't Broken, Don't Fix It

If your phone, laptop, or television still works, then why would you pay a considerable fee to replace it? Just because your phone operator offers you the chance to pay for a new phone each year does not mean you have to take it.

Use Systems to Your Advantage

Be savvy—use systems already in place to your advantage: tax-deferred investments, CollegeCounts 529, fiverr.com, business credit cards, Small Business Administration loans, and government grants—these things can save you a chunk of money in the long run. If something is provided to reward you, then you would be a fool not to accept that

reward with open arms!

You can't make decisions based on fear

and the possibility of what might happen.

– Michelle Obama